YOUNG ARCHITECT

Futuristic Homes

by Saranne Taylor

Illustrated by Moreno Chiacchiera and Michelle Todd

Crabtree Publishing Company

Crabtree Publishing Company

www.crabtreebooks.com
1-800-387-7650

Published in Canada
616 Welland Ave.
St. Catharines, ON
L2M 5V6

Published in the United States
PMB 59051, 350 Fifth Ave.
59th Floor,
New York, NY

Published in 2015 by CRABTREE PUBLISHING COMPANY.

Author: Saranne Taylor
Illustrators: Moreno Chiacchiera, Michelle Todd
Project coordinator: Kelly McNiven
Editor: Shirley Duke
Proofreader: Crystal Sikkens
**Production coordinator
      and prepress technician:** Ken Wright
Print coordinator: Katherine Berti

Photographs:
Pg 4 – Frank Boston
Pg 8 – (l) ArchMan (r) alexmillos
Pg 9 – wavebreakmedia
Pg 10 – (tl) Martin Bilek (tr) Christian Mueller
      (b) ecoventurestravel
Pg 11 - Tengbom.com / Bertil Hertzberg
Pg 13 - Nick Neyland / Flickr
Pg 14 – Algol
Pg 15 – (t) And Inc (b) Borna_Mirahmadian
Pg 17 – (main) SergeyDV (b) Chernetskiy
Pg 22 – (t) Karim Rashid Studio
      (b) Victor Vetterlein
Pg 23 - Photography of Dionisio González,
      courtesy of Yusto/Giner
Pg 24 - Mark Werner Hamilton / Flickr
Pg 26 – (main) andrey_I (insert) andrey_I

All images are Shutterstock.com unless otherwise stated.

Every attempt has been made to clear copyright. Should there be any inadvertent omissions, please notify the publisher.

Printed in Hong Kong/082014/BK20140613

Library and Archives Canada Cataloguing in Publication

Taylor, Saranne, author
      Futuristic homes / written by Saranne Taylor ; illustrated by Moreno Chiacchiera and Michelle Todd.

(Young architect)
Issued in print and electronic formats.
ISBN 978-0-7787-1439-2 (bound).--ISBN 978-0-7787-1455-2 (pbk.).--
ISBN 978-1-4271-1578-2 (pdf).--ISBN 978-1-4271-1574-4 (html)

      1. Dwellings--Juvenile literature. I. Chiacchiera, Moreno, illustrator
II. Todd, Michelle, 1978-, illustrator III. Title.

TH4811.5.T39 2014   j728   C2014-903745-7
                                                            C2014-903746-5

Library of Congress Cataloging-in-Publication Data

Taylor, Saranne, author.
 Futuristic homes / by Saranne Taylor ; illustrated by Moreno Chiacchiera and Michelle Todd.
      pages cm. -- (Young architect)
 Includes index.
 ISBN 978-0-7787-1439-2 (reinforced library binding) -- ISBN 978-0-7787-1455-2 (pbk.)
-- ISBN 978-1-4271-1578-2 (electronic pdf) -- ISBN 978-1-4271-1574-4 (electronic html)
 1. Architecture, Domestic--Forecasting--Juvenile literature. 2. Dwellings--Forecasting--Juvenile literature. I. Chiacchiera, Moreno, illustrator. II. Todd, Michelle, 1978- illustrator. III. Title.

 NA7120.T39 2014
 728.01'12--dc23
                                    2014020964

Contents

Introduction

Architects are working differently than in the past. They're using new building materials such as "bendy" concrete. They're creating fantastic designs with amazing new computer technology. Plans show homes run by computers, and buildings that are taller and stranger-looking than ever. We describe these designs as futuristic, meaning they use ideas and **engineering** that will be available in the future.

Cube house

Futuristic homes come in all shapes and sizes. Architects are thinking up ideas that seem unbelievable!

This house seems impossible! It looks like a set of blocks just stuck on to a tower. However the architect who created the design knows it can work because of the specific building **materials** and technology he's used.

The exciting thing about being a future architect is that almost any idea you come up with will probably be possible. You can let your imagination run wild!

A cube house - a futuristic design

The rooms

All the rooms in the cube house are in separate block shapes, joined together with stairs.

Some of the cubes have moving walls or floors to change the shape inside the rooms and create more space.

All the electrical equipment is powered by **remote control**, like your television, or by special computers that recognize your face or fingerprints. You can even turn on your shower this way.

The two cubes at the top can move up and down on mechanical levers. These work like a robot's arms.

There is a private cube for guests which can be moved away from the house on tracks, and an underground cube for children to play in.

There's an elevator, which moves inside a tunnel, or shaft. It rises through the middle of the building to the **helipad** on the roof.

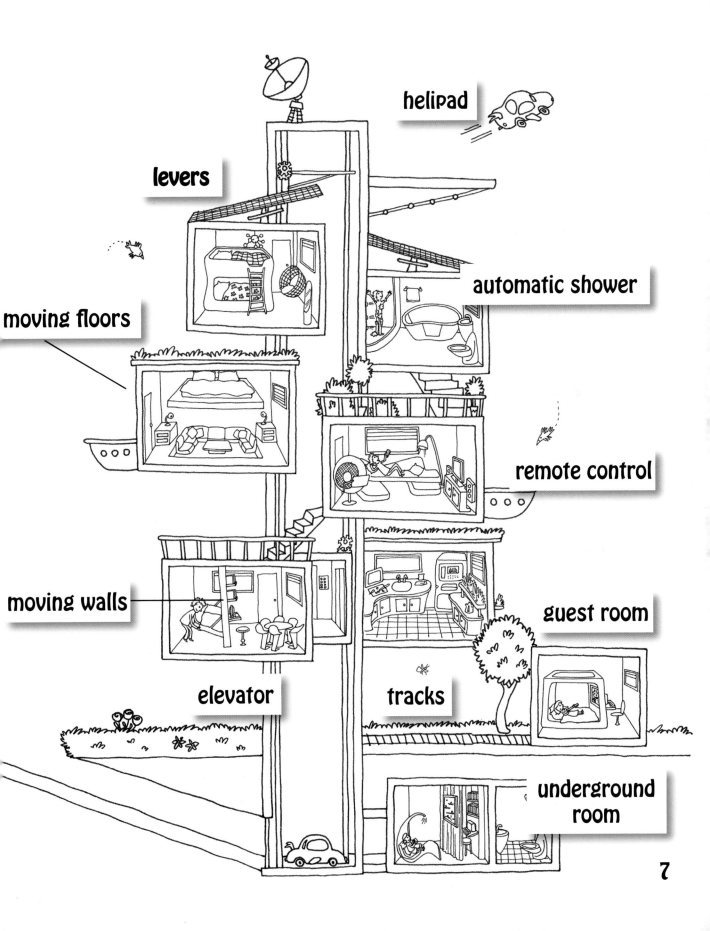

helipad

levers

automatic shower

moving floors

remote control

moving walls

guest room

elevator

tracks

underground room

7

Designing the future computers...

What sort of equipment does an architect need?
A pen or pencil and some paper to make notes and sketches will come in handy.

But today, almost all architects are using computers to create their designs. This special technology is called CAD, or Computer Aided Design.

A CAD floor plan of a building

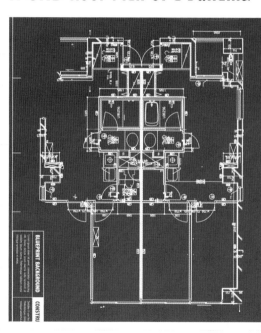

A CAD model of a city skyline

It helps the architect draw a concept, or idea, with the exact measurements needed. Then this important information can be passed on to the builder.

...and holographs

But CAD can only create a picture on your computer screen. It can only show two-dimensional, or 2-D, drawings that are flat, like they'd appear in a book. But imagine a computer which can create pictures like those in a pop-up book—images which appear solid!

An architect and a builder using a holograph design

Holographs can create these three-dimensional, or 3-D, models. Architects can now show their concept as if it were a mini-version of the real thing. People can see all sides of the model, not just the front. They can also see behind the building, above it, and even inside!

Running out of space!

Every day, the number of people in the world is growing, and everyone needs somewhere to live. The problem is the planet isn't getting any bigger and we're running out of space!

Architects must design homes that provide us with **shelter**, but don't take up too much room.

CONTAINER APARTMENTS
These homes are made from old shipping containers, stacked on top of each other just like children's building blocks!

CLOSE-FITTING LEANERS
Some designs seem to squeeze the houses together to fit in as many as possible.

UNDERGROUND HOUSING
And when there isn't any room left on top—we can always build under the ground!

POD LIVING

Sometimes you don't need a lot of space to live. You just need to design it well.

These little pod houses are only a few yards (meters) long, but they have a kitchen, bathroom, and a living area with lots of space for storage.

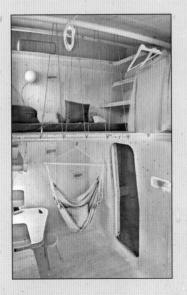

They even have a second floor with a tiny staircase leading to a bedroom.

Area and volume

Architects have to think carefully when they design a building. One of the most important things they think about is its shape and how much space it takes up.

octagon

An octagon is an eight-sided shape. It is used in architecture all over the world. This is because a design with so many sides gives the building lots of space inside. Also, it has more walls than a normal square home, so you can put in more windows and create more light.

Design a shape home

Draw your own **floor plan** for a house using a shape as your starting point.

1. Draw the basic shape.
2. Decide how many bedrooms you will need for your family.
3. Add them to your plan, along with a kitchen and bathroom.
4. What other rooms do you need?
5. Don't forget space for your hobbies and your pets!

star home

triangle home

kite-shaped home

A many-sided home

The design of this home is based on the shape of an octagon. This gives the house lots of interesting angles and views in all directions.

Communal living

One way to create more space for families is to build homes where people can live close together. We call this a **community**. In this way, people can share public transportation, stores, schools, hospitals, and other public buildings.

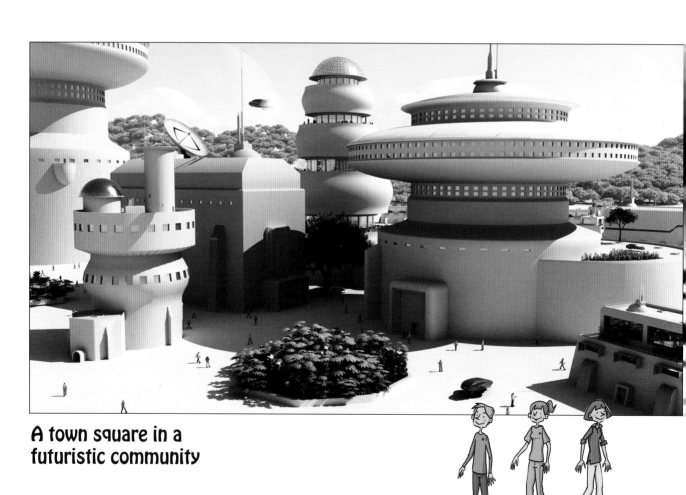

A town square in a futuristic community

A model of a futuristic city full of skyscrapers

Architects are designing cities of the future that create communities. They often include tall skyscrapers or buildings that can house hundreds of families. In fact, the skyline in Dubai, in the United Arab Emirates, is already starting to look like an architect's futuristic **model**!

The skyline of Dubai

New materials

If you're going to make a futuristic home, you're going to need some futuristic materials. You could use these:

AEROGEL - This is a mixture of air and a type of soft gel. It's sometimes called solid smoke because that's what it looks like. It's very strong, makes really good **insulation**, and helps keep the temperature inside a building at a constant level.

BENDY CONCRETE - Usually concrete is a hard, gray material made from a mixture of water, cement, and crushed rocks. BUT, in the future you'll be able to bend it and even see right through it. It will last forever because it can be repaired by just adding water!

TRANSPARENT ALUMINUM - This is a metal, but you can see through it! It's very strong, but light and bendable at the same time.

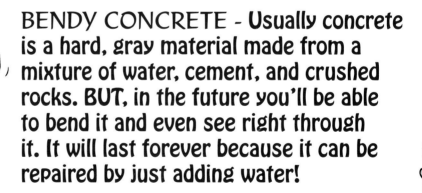

This futuristic house uses all these kinds of materials:

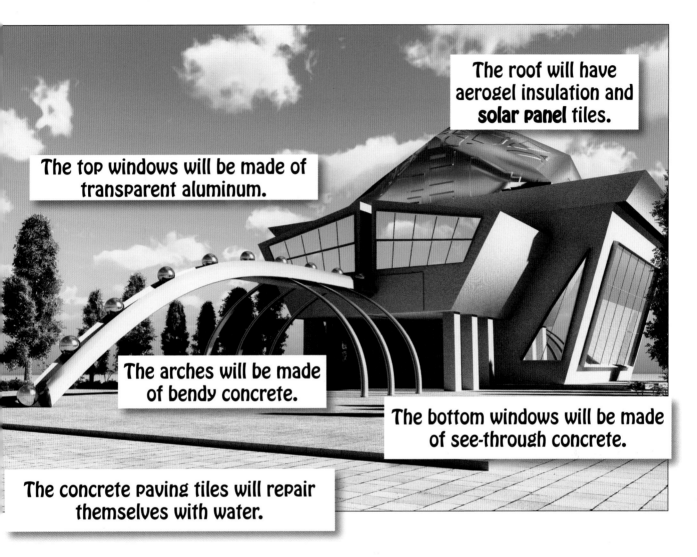

The roof will have aerogel insulation and **solar panel** tiles.

The top windows will be made of transparent aluminum.

The arches will be made of bendy concrete.

The bottom windows will be made of see-through concrete.

The concrete paving tiles will repair themselves with water.

3-D PRINTING—Architects also have plans to use amazing technology to build their designs. They will soon be able to use a special machine called a 3-D printer which is able to print a solid **structure** straight from the computer.

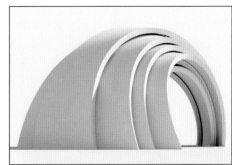

A 3-D printer created this bendy concrete house. 17

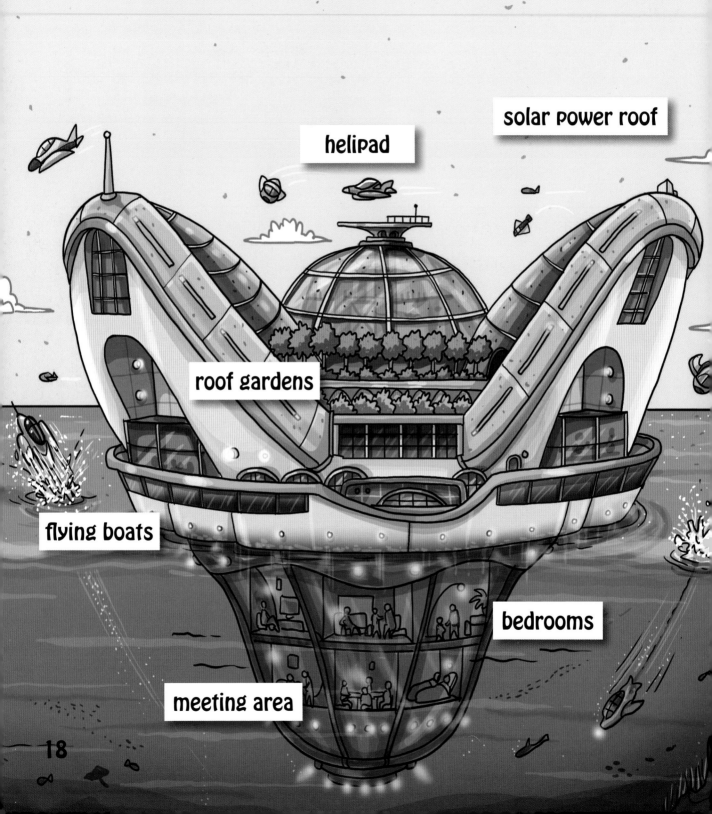

solar power roof

helipad

roof gardens

flying boats

bedrooms

meeting area

18

In the sea!

What would it be like to live under the ocean? How would life be different?

This undersea village is a small community that has everything you need.

People live in apartments below the water, which are small but well-designed.

Stores, businesses, schools, restaurants, libraries, and doctors are all available within one structure.

Gardens and parks are on the roof of the building.

A boat, a plane, or a helicopter—or maybe even a futuristic flying boat—can take people to see their friends and family or bring them to the mainland.

The village can either be anchored to the same spot, or float freely in the sea. It can also be sailed like a ship to visit other places.

Living underwater

Living under the sea is something that might be possible in the future. Architects have already made several detailed plans.

Like a skyscraper, a seascraper is a tall building with a lot of apartments. But the difference is ... it will be several stories DEEP instead of several stories TALL!

It will house hundreds of families and only the top few levels of the building will be above the water!

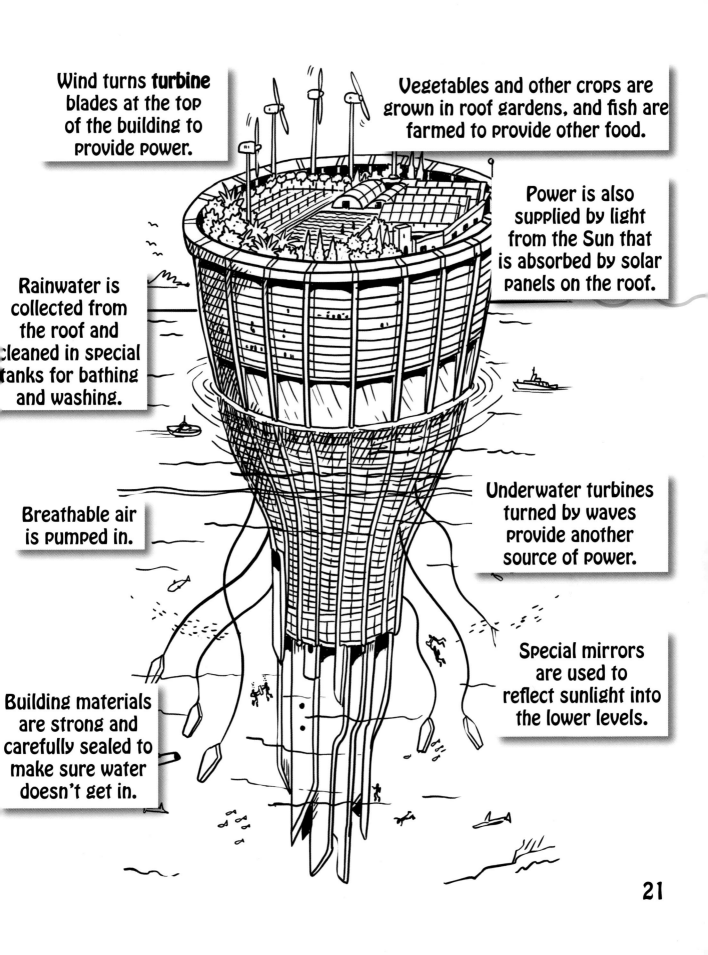

Wind turns **turbine** blades at the top of the building to provide power.

Vegetables and other crops are grown in roof gardens, and fish are farmed to provide other food.

Power is also supplied by light from the Sun that is absorbed by solar panels on the roof.

Rainwater is collected from the roof and cleaned in special tanks for bathing and washing.

Breathable air is pumped in.

Underwater turbines turned by waves provide another source of power.

Building materials are strong and carefully sealed to make sure water doesn't get in.

Special mirrors are used to reflect sunlight into the lower levels.

Safe and friendly

Our environment, the place where we live, is in danger because people are not taking care of it. Because of this, architects have begun to create designs that are better for the planet.

Eco-homes of the future

- Architect's words
Eco-friendly
Eco is short for ecology, which is the study of how animals live in their environment. Being eco-friendly means using materials that are safe for our planet or made from natural products.

These futuristic homes have been designed as **eco-friendly** buildings. They are powered using specially designed systems that avoid harmful-to-the-environment methods of heating and cooling. They use the power of the Sun and wind to provide all of their electricity.

22

Our planet suffers from many kinds of natural disasters—earthquakes, tornadoes, hurricanes, tsunamis, and flooding. These events aren't always predictable, so we often don't know when they're going to happen.

- Architect's words -
Disaster proof
Designs of the future will have to provide buildings with protection from natural disasters. They will need to be made of very tough materials that can stand up to strong winds, high water levels, and sudden or violent shaking of the ground.

Building designed to withstand natural disasters

Architects understand this problem and are now creating special designs which will survive in such difficult situations.

Dome shelter

Homes are also shelters. They must be built to protect the people inside. One of the safest and most eco-friendly designs is a monolithic dome.

A monolithic dome in Texas

Monolithic describes a building which is made in one piece. This makes it much stronger and safer in case of a natural disaster. During tornadoes and hurricanes, the powerful winds are forced underneath the building causing them to weaken. In an earthquake, the dome will move with the ground so it won't collapse.

1. Building a monolithic dome begins with a circle of concrete to create a solid base or **foundation**. Then, a kind of tent is filled with air, or inflated, to form the shape of the structure.

2. Once the tent is completely inflated, it is covered with a metal criss-cross **frame** to give it strength.

3. A special kind of foam is sprayed on the inside for insulation. Then, concrete is sprayed on the outside to make it weather-proof.

4. Finally, the finished structure is painted.

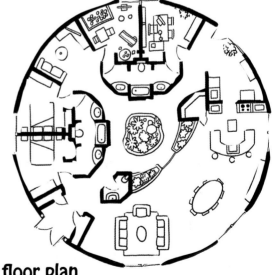

5. This floor plan shows the design of the inside of the dome.

Apartments which spiral into the sky

A skyscraper with 1,000 stories

Climbing cities

But what if there's no room left on land or in the sea? We will have to move upward into the sky. Imagine a skyscraper that has one thousand stories and goes way above the clouds!

Another futuristic concept is part home and part flying machine! The three-story house dangles from strong cables attached to two huge balloons. It has large windows on all sides and an open-air deck so the views are great. Inside, everything is run by remote control.

And you can travel anywhere!

Another planet!

In the future, there may be whole cities of people living in outer space. However, first new technologies have to be invented which will make it easier to live there.

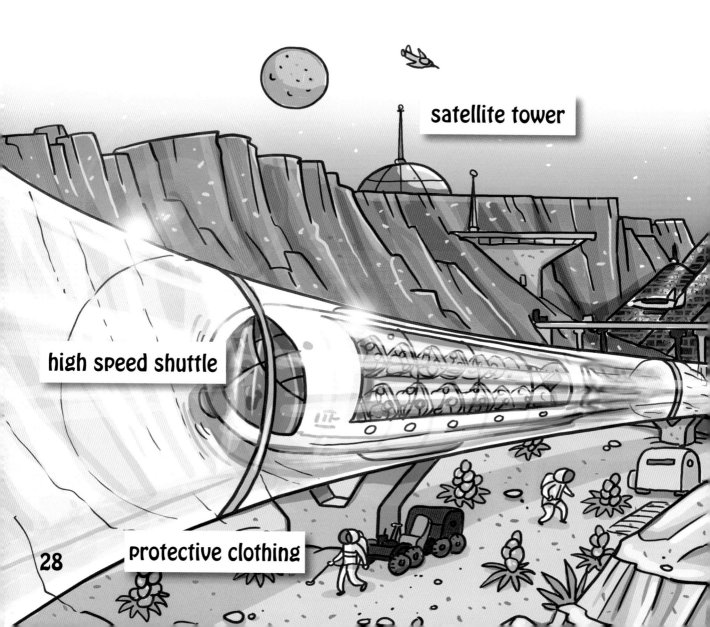

satellite tower

high speed shuttle

protective clothing

We will need intelligently designed buildings and futuristic transportation to get around. Breathable air will have to be pumped in to make sure we can live. We will grow new types of food to eat, and whenever we go outside, we'll have to wear special suits.

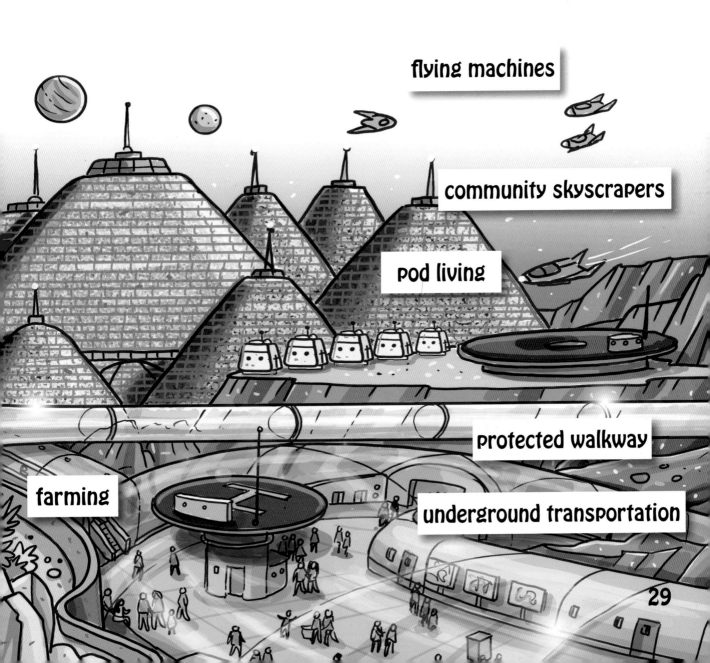

flying machines

community skyscrapers

pod living

protected walkway

farming

underground transportation

Glossary

community A place where families live close together with stores and services nearby

eco-friendly A description of something that is natural or not harmful to the environment

engineering Using math, science, and creative thinking to design things and solve problems

floor plan An outline drawing showing the layout and size of a building

foundation The solid base of a building, usually made from concrete

frame A support to which parts of a building are attached

helipad A landing or take-off place for a helicopter, often on the roof of a building

holograph Three-dimensional pictures created by a computer

insulation Materials applied to the walls of a building which help protect the inside of the building from changing temperatures

lever A bar that rests on a support called a fulcrum which lifts or moves loads

materials Things used to construct a home

model An exact copy of the actual building shrunk down and used as a guide

remote control A tool which controls equipment from a distance using special signals

shelter Something that covers and protects a person or animal from the weather

solar panel A specially treated plate mounted on a frame that collects sunlight and changes it into electricity

structure Another name for the framework of a building

turbine A set of blades turned by wind or moving water that can be used to produce electricity

Learning more

Books:

Laroche, Giles. *If You Lived Here: Houses of the World.* New York, NY: HMH Books for Young Readers, 2011.
This book traces homes around the world and the ways people have adapted their homes to fit the way they live and their environment.

McLeish, Ewan. *Sustainable Homes.* Mankato, MN: Smart Apple Media, 2006.
This book explains how creating sustainable homes helps make changes in the way people think about homes.

Royston, Angela. *Buildings of the Future.* Chicago, IL: Heinemann Raintree, 2007.
Read about the designs and new developments in buildings and how they will fit into our environment in the future, as well as how old structures can be adapted.

Websites:

www.forbes.com/pictures/elfk45ifj/tornado-proof-home/#gallerycontent
View different furturistic home designs and see how their architecture will help make life easier.

www.colorcoat-online.com/blog/index.php/2011/05/17-futuristic-eco-homes/
Discover 17 futuristic eco-homes from around the world. Some are already built and others are still in the planning stage.

www.futuristicarchitecturedesign.us/
Visit images of futuristic homes--already here and built--and read a short paragraph about how the materials help make them what they are.

Index